P9-AQE-458

Horses, Horses, Horses

By Allan Fowler

Consultants:
Robert L. Hillerich, Ph.D., Bowling Green
State University, Bowling Green, Ohio

Mary Nalbandian, Director of Science,
Chicago Public Schools, Chicago, Illinois

Fay Robinson, Child Development Specialist

CHILDRENS PRESS ®
CHICAGO

Design by Beth Herman Design Associates

Library of Congress Cataloging-in-Publication Data

Fowler, Allan
     Horses, horses, horses / by Allan Fowler.
       p. cm. –(Rookie read-about science)
     Summary: a simple explanation of how horses are beautiful and
useful animals.
     ISBN 0-516-14921-6
     1. Horses–Juvenile literature. [1. Horses.] I. Title.
   II. Series: Fowler, Allan. Rookie read-about science.
SF302.F68 1992
636.1–dc20   91-35063
                                                  CIP
                                                   AC

How did people get around before there were any cars?

Before there were any planes or trains or buses?

Horses!

When people didn't walk, they rode on horseback. Or in coaches or open carriages, wagons or streetcars pulled by horses.

Horses, horses, horses crowded the streets of cities and towns.

Horses pulled farmers' plows.

Now tractors pull the plows.

But horses are still
important today—
in other ways.

People ride them for fun.

Or enjoy horse races and polo, a game played on horseback.

Trained horses perform in circuses and horse shows.

Horses help cowboys
and mounted police
do their jobs.

Horses can be as small as
this tiny Shetland pony...

or as big as this
Clydesdale, a horse that
can do heavy work.

Every horse has a mane,
the row of hair along its
neck.

A baby horse, or foal, can stand up almost as soon as it is born.

A young female horse is
called a filly. She grows
up to become a mare.

A young male horse is called a colt. He grows up to become a stallion.

Did you know that most
horses wear shoes?

The shoes protect the horse's hoofs.

A blacksmith nails the horseshoes to the horse's hoofs so they won't come off.

This doesn't hurt the horse.

Horses live in buildings called stables when they aren't working.

Their owners must give
them plenty of exercise,
water, and food.

Dinner for a horse might
be hay or other grasses,
oats and corn.

Horses are beautiful
animals and loyal friends.

Can you imagine what
it was like a long,
long time ago–

when people had a
family horse instead
of a family car?

Words You Know

horses

filly   mare   colt

mane

foal

Clydesdale

Shetland pony

blacksmith   horseshoes

stable

Index

About the Author

Allan Fowler is a free-lance writer with a background in advertising. Born in New York, he lives in Chicago now and enjoys traveling.

Photo Credits

Animals Animals – ©Fritz Prenzel, 14, 31 (top right)

North Wind Picture Archives – 4, 7

SuperStock International, Inc. – 28-29; ©Bob F. Ozment, 12

©Sarah Hoskins – Temple Farms, Home of the Lipizzans, Wadsworth, Illinois, 24, 31 (bottom right)

Valan – ©J. Eascott/V. Momatiuk, Cover; ©Clara Parsons, 8; ©Kennon Cooke, 9, 15, 31 (top left); Phillip Norton, 10; ©Y.R. Tymstra, 11; ©Stephen J. Krasemann, 13; ©Francis Lepine, 16, 30 (bottom left); ©Herman H. Giethoorn, 19, 30 (bottom right); ©John Fowler, 20, 22, 30 (top left), 31 (bottom left); ©Alan Wilkinson, 21, 30 (top right); ©J.A.Wilkinson, 25, 26; ©John Cancalosi, 27

COVER: Horses and flowers